AROUND THE WORLD IN...

1500

AROUND THE WORLD IN...

1500

by Virginia Schomp

BENCHMARK BOOKS

MARSHALL CAVENDISH
NEW YORK

With thanks to J. Brett McClain of the Oriental Institute,
the University of Chicago, for his careful reading of the manuscript

Benchmark Books
Marshall Cavendish Corporation
99 White Plains Road
Tarrytown, New York 10591-9001
www.marshallcavendish.com

• • •

Library of Congress Cataloging-in-Publication Data
Schomp, Virginia
1500/Virginia Schomp
p. cm—(Around the world in— ; 1)
Includes bibliographical references and index.
ISBN 0-7614-1082-1
Summary: Surveys important occurrences in Europe, Africa,
Asia, and the Americas around the year 1500.
1. Discoveries in geography—Juvenile literature. 2. Explorers—Juvenile literature.
3. Sixteenth century—Juvenile literature. 4. Civilization, Medieval—Juvenile literature.
[1. World history. 2. Fifteenth century.] I. Title. II. Series.
D208.A47 2001 909'.5—dc21 00-041449

• • •

Printed in Italy
1 3 5 6 4 2

• • •

Book Designer: Judith Turziano
Photo Research: Rose Corbett Gordon, Mystic CT

• • •

half title: An Aztec goldsmith in his shop, from an account written
and illustrated by Bernardino de Sahagun, a sixteenth-century Spaniard.
title page: The *Pinta*, the *Niña*, and the *Santa Maria* journey
to the Americas in this nineteenth-century lithograph.

• • •

CREDITS
Front cover: (top) Bettmann/Corbis; (bottom left) Dallas and John Heaton/Corbis;
(bottom right) Werner Forman/Art Resource, NY
Back cover: (top) Louvre, Paris, France/Bridgeman Art Library; (bottom) The Art Archive

Page 1, 42: Biblioteca Medicea-Laurenziana, Florence, Italy/Bridgeman Art Library;
page 2, 19, 22: Private Collection/Index/Bridgeman Art Library; page 3: Erich Lessing/Art Resource, NY;
page 6: Bargello, Florence, Italy/Bridgeman Art Library; page11, 12: Scala/Art Resource, NY;
page 13: Louvre, Paris, France/Bridgeman Art Library; page 14: Vatican Museums and Galleries, Vatican
City, Italy/Bridgeman Art Library; page 15: Galleria dell'Accademia, Florence, Italy/Bridgeman Art Library;
page 17, 20-21: Bettmann/Corbis; page 25: Sovfoto; page 26: Sovfoto/Eastfoto; page 29: Private Collection/The Stapleton
Collection/Bridgeman Art Library; page 33, 34, 35, 36, 50, 61, 65, 68, 70, 83, 88: The Granger Collection, New York;
page 39, 53: The Art Archive; page 40-41: Bridgeman Art Library; page 44-45: Private Collection/Ian Mursell/Mexicolore/
Bridgeman Art Library; page 47: Danny Lehman/Corbis; page 49: Art Resource, NY; page 54: Biblioteca del ICI, Madrid,
Spain/Index/Bridgeman Art Library; page 59, 62: Giraudon/Art Resource, NY; page 67: Dallas and John Heaton/Corbis;
page 71: Maidstone Museum and Art Gallery, Kent, UK/Bridgeman Art Library; page 74: Bonhams, London,
UK/Bridgeman Art Library; page 75: Sakamoto Photo Research Laboratory/Corbis; page 79, 80, 85, 86:
Werner Forman/Art Resource, NY; page 87: British Museum, London, UK/Bridgeman Art Library.

CONTENTS

Kind David, with the head of the giant Goliath at his feet. Andrea del Verrocchio, the Italian Renaissance artist, expressed the new philosophy of humanism in this work. David's muscles and the expression on his face are realistically sculpted, drawn from the artist's knowledge of human anatomy. A later Renaissance sculptor, Michelangelo, would take the human form to even greater heights.

INTRODUCTION

The time is around A.D. 1500. In what is now Mexico, the emperor of a vast civilization ponders signs that seem to predict the coming of strange warriors. Far to the east, in Japan, a troubled shogun withdraws from the world to seek peace through Buddhist meditation. On the west coast of Africa, the people of the kingdom of Benin are recording their history on exquisite bronze plaques. And in the newly unified nation of Spain, a queen is wondering if a ship really could reach the riches of the East by sailing west, across the Sea of Darkness.

If you could board a time machine and get off at 1500, these are some of the events you might witness. Most people learn about history by focusing on just one country or place. Usually they learn about events only from their own perspective, that is, from the point of view of their nation or heritage. This is certainly a valid way to try to understand the world, but it can also be narrow and one-sided. In this book we thought it might be worthwhile to take a different approach to history, by looking at events that were occurring all across the world at one period of time. Around 1500, for example, a sculptor and painter named Michelangelo cast aside the medieval idea that the only acceptable purpose of art was to praise God. Artists, he thought, might also create works that glorified the human spirit. Michelangelo's art was inspired by a new philosophy, a new way of looking at the world, called humanism. He was part of the reawakening of knowledge and culture in western Europe that became known as the Renaissance. But change and "progress" were happening in other parts of the world while Michelangelo was at work. In this book we try to take a broader, "bird's-eye" view of history, so that all of us may be able to understand one another better.

EUROPE
AROUND 1500

North Sea

Baltic Sea

IRELAND

ENGLAND

FRANCE

Bay of Biscay

Venice
Genoa
Florence
Rome

Adriatic Sea

PORTUGAL

LEÓN

ARAGON

Madrid
CASTILE

SPAIN

Granada

Tyrrhenian Sea

Mediterranean Sea

Atlantic Ocean

Novgorod
Moscow

Ugra River

Volga River

Volga River

Caspian Sea

Black Sea

Constantinople
(Istanbul)

Aegean Sea

N
W   E
S

■ IVAN THE GREAT'S EMPIRE

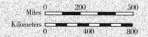

Miles   0   200   500
Kilometers 0   400   800

PART I

EUROPE

Five hundred years ago the map of Europe looked quite different from the way it looks today. Instead of well-organized, powerful nations like those of modern times, much of the continent was divided up among various kingdoms, city-states, and private territories ruled by nobles. In what would become the nation of Italy, city-states competed against one another for power and wealth. Germany, too, was not yet unified. Made up of independent territories, it was torn by political and religious strife. In parts of Hungary, Greece, and the Balkan Peninsula, foreign conquerors ruled. Despite all this conflict, Europe was about to enter a glorious age of learning and exploration. Young artists in the city-state of Florence, encouraged by a wealthy banker, were expressing bold new ideas. A historic voyage of discovery was made possible by monarchs in newly unified Spain. And to the east the grand duke of Moscow had transformed a small city into a great empire.

WHEN THEY RULED

In Florence, The House of Medici
c. 1360–1737

In Spain, The Age of Isabella and Ferdinand
1469–1516

In Russia, The Empire of the Czars
1500–1917

IN FLORENCE

LORENZO DE' MEDICI ENCOURAGES THE ARTS

Lorenzo de' Medici strolled through the garden beside his palace in the Italian city-state of Florence. He was admiring the work of the students in his school for artistic boys. Lorenzo had supplied some of his own antique statues for the boys to use as models. Among these was the stone figure of an aged faun, a half human, half animal mythological creature with horns like a goat. Lorenzo paused in surprise beside the figure and the new student who was copying it, Michelangelo Buonarroti.

Although he had never touched a chisel before, Michelangelo had carved an incredibly accurate copy of the faun's head—but he had added something. He had carved an open mouth, complete with tongue and teeth. Laughing, Lorenzo asked, "Don't you know that old people never have all their teeth? Some are always missing."

The man moved on, leaving the student to carefully consider his work. Finally Michelangelo broke off one of the carved teeth. Then he hollowed out the gum to look as if the tooth had fallen out. Would the school's patron return and notice?

Lorenzo did return, and he was delighted with the imagination the boy had shown in aging the face of the sculpture. The wealthy man took the young artist into his home and, until his patron's death in 1492, Michelangelo ate at the Medici family table and showed Lorenzo his work every day.

Lorenzo de' Medici was the head of a family of wealthy merchants and bankers who controlled the city-state of Florence. Today scholars tell us that Florence is where the Renaissance began. *Renaissance* is a French word meaning "rebirth." Around 1400 Italian scholars became interested

Lorenzo de' Medici was famous throughout Europe for his love of the arts. The Florentine leader's generous support of Renaissance writers, scholars, and artists earned him the title Lorenzo the Magnificent.

in the classical world—the world of the ancient Greeks and Romans. During the Middle Ages many of the ideas and advances of those ancient civilizations had been forgotten. Now they were "reborn" as scholars took a new look at classical ideas and began to develop them in entirely new directions.

Nowhere was the excitement of Renaissance times greater than in Florence. In this large and prosperous city, followers of a new philosophy called humanism rejected the medieval Church's strict control of knowledge and the arts. The humanists embraced the classical idea that people should be free to examine the world around them and discover their own truths. Humanist scholars studied classical texts and wrote brilliant new works of poetry, philosophy, and science. Painters and sculptors worked out new methods for creating dramatic, realistic images of people and nature. Architects used classical techniques to fill Florence with buildings as

During the Renaissance, Florence was a vibrant center of trade, learning, and the arts. The Arno River, which runs through the center of the city, provided freshwater, energy, and a link to other thriving Italian city-states.

The Mona Lisa, *painted around 1503, represented Leonardo da Vinci's vision of ideal beauty. Centuries later, people still debate the meaning of her mysterious smile.*

glorious as any in ancient Rome. Leonardo da Vinci, perhaps the greatest Renaissance genius, experimented with new ways of seeing the world, not only through art and architecture but also as a musician, scientist, and engineer. His works included the famous paintings the *Mona Lisa* and the *Last Supper*, as well as plans for city streets and sketches of futuristic inventions—a tank, a submarine, parachutes, even a human-powered flying machine.

The Renaissance flowering of knowledge and the arts was made possible by the wealthy patrons who paid for all this work. Patrons like the Medici family, hoping to gain God's favor as well as glory for themselves and their city, sponsored the efforts of scholars, artists, and architects. Lorenzo de' Medici's school for boys was just one example of the many ways Florentine patrons encouraged and supported the arts. That school's most famous student, Michelangelo Buonarroti, went on to outshine his teachers. Although he was a master at the techniques of classical art, Michelangelo often ignored the rules, fudging realism to better show humanity's pure and noble spirit. In 1504 he sculpted the eighteen-foot-tall statue *David*, a powerful image of

In this scene from Michelangelo's ceiling of the Sistine Chapel, God reaches out to give Adam the spark of life.

physical perfection. His magnificent mural on the ceiling of the Sistine Chapel in Rome, which covers nearly six thousand square feet and took four years to complete, is considered one of the world's greatest artistic accomplishments.

The work of Michelangelo and other artists and scholars around 1500 reflected a new curiosity about the world as well as the courage to explore new possibilities. Renaissance ideas would spread north, to the rest of Europe, influencing Western thought well into the seventeenth century. And that same adventurous spirit would inspire a bold Italian explorer to make a journey that would transform the history of the world.

Michelangelo's celebrated marble statue of David, king of Israel, holds a slingshot over his shoulder, ready to slay the biblical giant Goliath. When one Italian writer saw the statue, he exclaimed, "Anyone who has seen Michelangelo's David has no need to see anything else by any other sculptor, living or dead."

IN SPAIN

CHRISTOPHER COLUMBUS DREAMS OF THE SEA

While Michelangelo was growing up in Florence, Christopher Columbus of Genoa, another city-state on the Italian peninsula, was earning his living sailing on merchant ships to Iceland and West Africa. Much of the world was still unexplored in the late 1400s. Although the ancient Greeks had known that the world was round, many medieval Europeans believed it was flat. Contact with Arab scholars in the eleventh century began to change those ideas. By the 1400s most Europeans accepted the notion of a round world. Their new maps represented Europe fairly accurately and made a lopsided guess at Africa and Asia. But they showed the Atlantic Ocean stretching west all the way from Europe to Asia, with only a scattering of islands in between. Sailors feared the broad Atlantic. They called it the "Sea of Darkness" and believed it was filled with fearsome serpents, wild winds, and deadly whirlpools.

Still, traders were eager to find a reliable way to reach the riches of Cathay (China) and the Indies (not India, but a name merchants gave to the unknown lands in Asia that produced exotic spices). The long overland route—from Genoa or Venice across the Mediterranean Sea, through Constantinople (now Istanbul, Turkey) to Persia (Iran), and on to India and China—was difficult and dangerous. European navigators wondered if there might be another way to reach the Indies. Could they go by sea?

Columbus was convinced it could be done. Studying all the maps and books he could find, he hatched a plan to cross the Sea of Darkness, to "sail west to reach the East." When he described his plan to Paolo Toscanelli, a noted Florentine geographer, the man praised his "grand and noble desire." But it was one thing to convince a scholar. To make his dream a reality, Columbus needed ships and a crew. That called for royal support and

World maps in the 1400s showed only a vast sea between Europe and Asia, and stories circulated that the dark waters were filled with fantastic creatures.

financial backing, which proved nearly impossible to find. Columbus pitched his plan to King John II of Portugal, King Henry VII of England, and King Charles VIII of France, all with the same disappointing results. Then, in 1486, he took his dream to Queen Isabella.

Isabella had become queen of the ancient kingdoms of Castile and León in

THE RICHES OF ASIA

The Europeans of 1500 longed for the treasures of Asia. Europe had few gold mines, no silkworms to produce silk fiber, no warm seas where oysters yielded lustrous pearls. Yet of all the rare and wonderful treasures of the East, none was more highly valued than spices.

Pepper from the berries of the East Indian pepper plant. Cinnamon from the dried inner bark of Asian laurel trees. Ginger and nutmeg from the roots and seeds of trees found only in Asia. The spices of the East added flavor to the Europeans' boring diet, which consisted largely of bread, porridge, cabbages, and turnips. Spices also camouflaged the taste of meat gone bad from lack of refrigeration. In some places an ounce of pepper might cost more than an ounce of gold. Apothecaries weighing spices for sale closed their shop windows first, to prevent even a single precious grain from being blown away. So next time you eat cinnamon toast or pepper your eggs, remember that you would have considered yourself very fortunate indeed to eat so well if you had lived around 1500.

1474. A few years earlier, she had married Ferdinand of Aragon. Together they held much of what is now Spain. The remaining land was held by the Moors, followers of Islam from North Africa. Isabella and Ferdinand were determined to drive out the Moors. In 1492 they captured the enemies' last stronghold, the fortress city of Granada, and expelled the Moors from Spain. King Ferdinand and Queen Isabella found themselves rulers of a unified nation.

Columbus hoped that the monarchs' triumph would lead to a favorable decision on his proposal. Now that Spain had vanquished the Moors, it could afford to fund the expedition. And if Columbus were right, the voyage held the promise of rich trading opportunities for Spain. At last, six years after first hearing the explorer's plan, Queen Isabella was convinced. In April she and King Ferdinand signed an agreement appointing Columbus

The* Santa María *approaches the coast of the New World.
The hundred-foot-long vessel was the flagship of the tiny fleet
commanded by Columbus on his historic voyage of discovery.

admiral of "all islands and mainlands that shall be discovered by his effort…in the Ocean Seas."

On September 6, 1492, Columbus led his little fleet of three ships—the *Niña*, the *Pinta*, and the *Santa María*—westward into the unknown sea. As land disappeared, the crew became restless. No sailor had ever dared to navigate out of sight of land for more than a day, and it was scary going where no one had gone before. Columbus boasted that he could use his compass, sextant, and other navigational tools to determine their position

at sea. As days turned to weeks, however, the sailors weren't sure they believed him. On September 18 Martín Alonso Pinzón, captain of the *Pinta*, thought he saw land to the north. The crew wanted to change course, but Columbus refused. A week later land was again spotted on the distant horizon, but it turned out to be nothing but a mass of storm clouds. Some of the sailors began to grumble darkly about throwing the captain overboard and turning back.

On the morning of October 1, a pair of small birds flew over the ships. On

October 11 the *Niña*'s crew caught sight of a thorn branch covered with red berries, and sailors on the *Santa María* saw a stick bobbing in the water. Columbus was sure these were signs that they were nearing their destination at last. And about two hours after midnight on October 12, his faith was rewarded by the eager cry of a seaman on the *Pinta*—*"Tierra!"* ("Land!")

At daybreak the three ships dropped anchor, and the crew rowed to shore. There they were greeted by a group of

New shipbuilding techniques and navigational tools helped launch the Age of Exploration in the mid-1400s. This explorer is using an astrolabe, an instrument for measuring the position of the heavenly bodies, to plot the location of newly discovered lands.

In this picture, a nineteenth-century artist imagines what Columbus's landing on San Salvador might have been like. From behind some trees, the Taino look on as Columbus proudly claims their island for Spain.

friendly Native Americans. Even though the land was already inhabited, Columbus planted a flag and a cross, claiming it for Spain. He believed he had found a corner of the Indies, but in fact the strange new land was a small island in the Bahamas, off the southeastern tip of North America. The people who lived there, the Taino, called their homeland

Guananí. Columbus named it San Salvador ("Holy Savior").

For the next three months, Columbus explored the Bahamas and the nearby islands now known as Cuba and Hispaniola, seeking the golden treasures of the East. He traded with the Taino (still confused about his location, he called them "Indios," or Indians), exchanging glass beads and red seamen's caps for green parrots, cotton thread, and darts. The explorer admired the beauty of the islands' lush forests, sandy beaches, and brightly colored flowers, fish, and birds. He jotted down descriptions of the Taino's canoes, made from hollowed-out tree trunks, and the swinging woven beds they called *hamacas* ("hammocks"). He was also impressed with the herb called *tobacos*, which the island people twisted into a tight roll, inserted in one nostril, lit, and smoked. But, except for a few gold and pearl trinkets, there was no sign of the vast treasures Columbus had expected.

Just before Christmas the *Santa María* ran aground on a coral reef and had to be abandoned. Three weeks later Columbus turned his two remaining ships toward home. With him he brought a few Taino captives and some jeweled masks and gold rings—enough to convince the Spanish king and queen that he had indeed found new lands in the Indies. Given a hero's welcome, the explorer was honored with the title Lord Admiral of the Ocean Seas. News of his discovery spread, and all Europe joined in the excitement. Both Spain and Portugal were eager to colonize the new territories, and soon England, France, and the Netherlands would also claim portions of the "New World."

Columbus made three more voyages across the Sea of Darkness, exploring Puerto Rico, South America, and Central America before his death in 1506. All his life he believed that he had discovered the western route to the Indies. Though he never realized that dream, his voyage is remembered as one of the most important events in history. Columbus had stumbled upon a "new" continent—a vast land whose full extent would not be measured for centuries to come. His discovery opened up that world to colonization, exploitation, and conquest, changing both Europe and the Americas forever.

IN RUSSIA
IVAN THE GREAT GATHERS AN EMPIRE

Half a century before our 1500 date, the ruler of a small city-state in eastern Europe was creating an empire. Since the age of eight, Ivan III had been joint ruler with his father, Grand Duke Vasily II, of the city-state of Moscow. Vasily taught his son to value land. Land could be used to buy the loyalty and military services of the grand duke's subjects. During his rule, Vasily grew in wealth and power by increasing the land under Moscow's control. On his death in 1462, he divided his territories among his four sons, leaving his title to the oldest, Ivan III.

"Grand Duke of Moscow" had a nice ring to it, but Ivan knew that, in spite of his title, he was no more than a minor ruler. He dreamed of owning more land—enough to give him the power to defeat any foe. His goal was to transform Moscow into a great empire. Within a few years of his father's death, he had seized almost all of his brothers' lands. Next he set his sights on the neighboring city-state of Novgorod.

Novgorod controlled thousands of square miles of thinly populated wilderness in northern and western Russia. The city, seated on a waterway leading to the Baltic Sea, was a center of trade in wax and furs. But the Novgorod's leaders found it difficult to control their far-flung lands, and they were helpless in the face of Ivan's determined assault. In 1471 the grand duke's troops easily defeated the army of Novgorod. At first Ivan let the conquered city keep some of its independence. Novgorod's *veche*, or city council, would continue to govern under the *posadnik*, or mayor, who in turn would report to Moscow. In 1478, however, the city's leaders rebelled, and Ivan tightened his grip. Exiling the rebel leaders to regions far from home, he packed up the great bell used to summon the *veche* to

*Ivan the Great, grand duke of Moscow. Ivan freed
Russia from Mongol rule and built a mighty empire.*

their meetings and carted it off to Moscow. "The *veche* bell in my patrimony [inherited lands] shall not be," he announced. "A *posadnik* there shall not be, and I shall rule the entire state." Novgorod's vast lands—along with the wealth and services of its landowners—were now under Ivan's absolute command.

Over the next few years, Ivan III continued to push back the borders of his kingdom, gathering up new lands by any means possible: purchase, treaty, war. By 1480 he was strong enough to challenge the Mongols, conquerors from eastern Asia who had dominated Russia for 250 years. The once-mighty Mongol Empire was past its prime, disintegrating into small territories, bickered over by rival princes. When one Mongol prince sent his troops marching against Moscow, Ivan answered with his own forces. The two armies met at the Ugra River. For weeks they camped on opposite banks, each

In this scene from a sixteenth-century history book, Ivan the Great's troops approach the Ugra River. The sight of these determined forces was enough to chase the Mongol army from Russia.

A HEAVENLY DEBATE

While Ivan the Great was carving out an empire in Russia, Renaissance astronomers were pondering less worldly matters. The ancient Greeks had proposed different theories about the heavens. Some said that the sun was the center of the universe and the earth revolved around it, while others—most notably the second-century A.D. astronomer Ptolemy—believed that the sun and the planets revolved around the earth. In the Middle Ages the Church latched on to Ptolemy's theory. Religious leaders approved of the idea that the earth, the Church, and God were the center of the universe. But around 1500 Nicolaus Copernicus, a Polish mathematician and astronomer, began to question that idea. The numbers just didn't add up. Copernicus's calculations seemed to prove that the earth moved around the sun.

Afraid to challenge the Church's teachings, Copernicus wrote down his findings—then sat on them for more than twenty years. Finally, in 1543, just before he died, he published his papers. The Church quickly condemned Copernicus's shocking notions and placed his book on its list of forbidden writings. But the cat was out of the bag. Other astronomers saw the logic in Copernicus's theory and began working to prove it. In

reluctant to strike the first blow. Finally the attackers made a quiet retreat, marking the end of Mongol rule.

By 1500 Ivan III ruled an empire stretching nearly 55,000 square miles. He had great power and wealth, but he wanted something more: glory. Western Europe was reveling in the artistic and scientific advances of the Renaissance, and Ivan wanted to appear just as grand. He hired Italian architects to design a splendid new palace, bell tower, and three glorious cathedrals. He married Sophia, niece of the last Byzantine emperor, which gave him the right to add the fancy Byzantine double-headed eagle to his

Nicolaus Copernicus laid the foundation for modern astronomy with his discovery that all the planets, including the earth, revolve around the sun.

1632 the Italian astronomer Galileo used his newly invented telescope to confirm the Copernican system. The Church clamped down again, imprisoning Galileo and forcing him to deny his discovery. But according to some stories, after taking an oath to "wholly forsake the false opinion that...the earth is not the center of the world and moves," the intrepid astronomer added under his breath, "And yet it does move."

family crest. The marriage also gave him the right to be the first Russian ruler to take the title *czar,* or emperor.

Because of his great power, Ivan was resented by the Russian nobility, who resisted his rule. Bitter disputes kept the czar from ever building a unified nation; that task would fall to his grandson, known as Ivan the Terrible. But by the time of his death in 1505, Ivan III had tripled the size of his empire, bringing nearly all of the future nation of Russia under Moscow's control. For that achievement history has honored him with the title Ivan the Great.

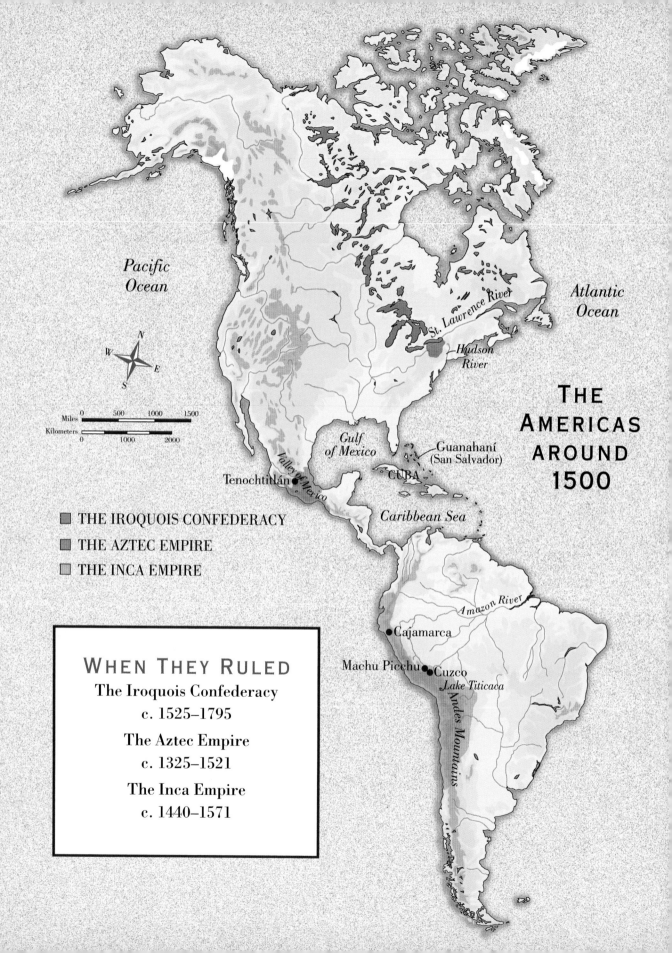

Pacific
Ocean

Atlantic
Ocean

St. Lawrence River

Hudson
River

THE
AMERICAS
AROUND
1500

Miles
0   500   1000   1500

Kilometers
0   1000   2000

Gulf
of Mexico

Guanahaní
(San Salvador)

Valley of Mexico

Tenochtitlán

CUBA

Caribbean Sea

THE IROQUOIS CONFEDERACY

THE AZTEC EMPIRE

THE INCA EMPIRE

Amazon River

Cajamarca

Machu Picchu ● Cuzco
Lake Titicaca

Andes Mountains

WHEN THEY RULED
The Iroquois Confederacy
c. 1525–1795

The Aztec Empire
c. 1325–1521

The Inca Empire
c. 1440–1571

PART II
THE AMERICAS

By the time Columbus reached the Americas in 1492, the New World was already home to millions of people, belonging to hundreds of different tribes. In the northwestern region of North America, the Haida people lived in wooden plank houses and fished for seafood, while the Sioux ranged across the Great Plains, hunting buffalo. The peaceful Cherokee raised crops and wove intricate baskets in the Southeast, while in the Southwest the warlike Navajo tended sheep and raided their Pueblo neighbors.

Although many tribes fought among themselves, some of the peoples of the Americas had created strong, united empires by 1500. But foreigners were about to arrive—not to meet the people who had shaped these remarkable civilizations but to conquer them.

THE IROQUOIS
THE PEOPLE OF THE LONGHOUSE MAKE PEACE

When Hiawatha's family was murdered by a rival chieftain, everyone expected him to take revenge. Instead, he found comfort in the words of a wise man known as the Peacemaker. Hiawatha and the Peacemaker traveled among the Onondaga, Mohawk, Cayuga, Oneida, and Seneca tribes. They urged the tribes to put an end to their constant wars, explaining that unity would make them strong. Many people saw the wisdom of this message, and four of the tribes agreed to attend a gathering to discuss peace.

Only Hiawatha's own people, the Onondaga, refused. The leader of the opposition was Tadodaho, a man so evil that serpents grew out of his head. Hiawatha combed the snakes from Tadodaho's hair, converting the leader to the ways of peace. Then he persuaded the Onondaga to join the other tribes by promising them the honor of serving as Keepers of the Central Fire. Once a year, tribal leaders agreed, they would gather around that fire to renew their vows of peace and unity. Together they swore an oath to "hold hands so tightly that a falling tree could not separate them." From then on, there was peace among the five tribes.

The legend of Hiawatha describes the birth of the Iroquois Confederacy. Around 1525 the five nations of the Hodenosaunee, or "People of the Longhouse" as the Iroquois called themselves, joined forced to form an alliance that would last for many years. The Iroquois lived in villages in northeastern North America, in what is now New York State. Their homes were wooden longhouses, which ranged in length from forty to two hundred feet. As many as twenty-four families might occupy a longhouse. Each family lived in its own space along one side of the house, sharing a cooking

Over the centuries, the Iroquois legend of Hiawatha has inspired many artists and writers. This engraving illustrated a nineteenth-century edition of Henry Wadsworth Longfellow's poem **The Song of Hiawatha.**

fire with the family on the opposite side. Small openings in the roof let sunlight in and smoke out.

Although the five tribes of the Hodenosaunee pledged to live in peace

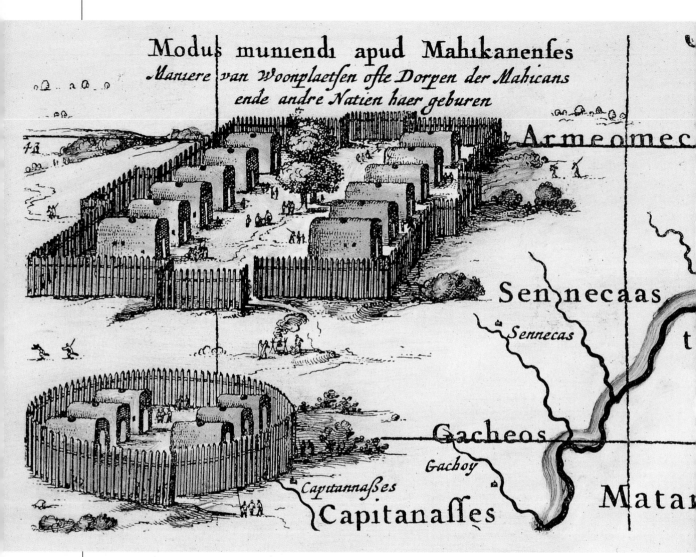

Modus muniendi apud Mahikanenses
Maniere van Woonplaetsen ofte Dorpen der Mahicans
ende andre Natien haer geburen

Armeomec

Sennecaas

Sennecas

Gacheos

Gachoy

Capitannaßes

Capitanaßes

Matar

In an Iroquois village, as many as one hundred longhouses might be grouped together inside palisades—fences made of long, pointed wooden stakes.

and unity with one another, that vow did not extend to tribes outside the confederacy. Iroquois war parties often attacked the villages of neighboring Algonquian and Huron tribes, sometimes to avenge a death, sometimes to gain personal glory, property, or captives. The victorious warriors brought home their captives, and the women decided what to do with them. Sometimes an enemy warrior was tortured and burned at the stake. More often the people adopted the captive into their tribe, especially if he was young and likely to accept Hodenosaunee ways. Adoptions helped the village fill the gaps left by warriors killed in battle.

Eventually the Iroquois would grow powerful and conquer all the Indian nations from the St. Lawrence River to Tennessee and from Maine to Michigan. But meetings with other tribes did not always end in warfare. The

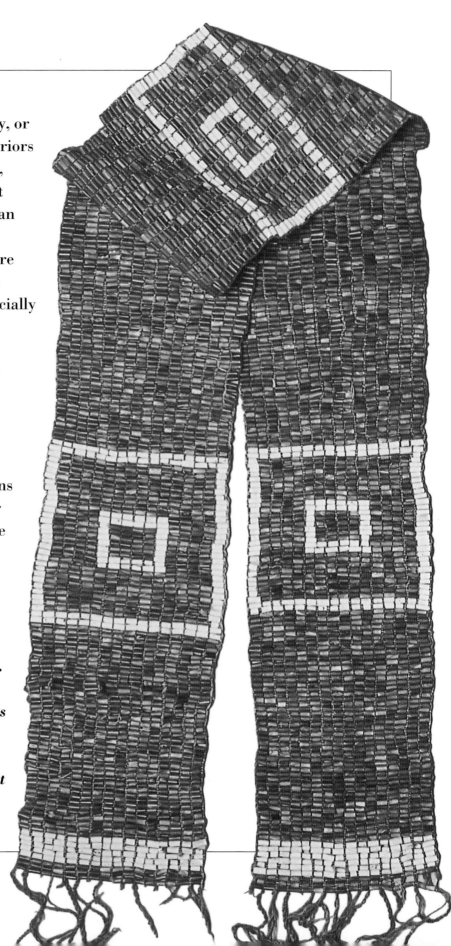

An Iroquois wampum belt. These belts of polished shell beads were sometimes used to communicate between tribes, with patterns woven to represent messages or agreements.

A Native American exchanges furs for a gun at a frontier trading post. At first, guns gave the Iroquois an advantage over other tribes, but in time close contact with Europeans brought conflict and destruction to the People of the Longhouse.

people of the Iroquois Confederacy traded with many other North American tribes, exchanging their food, clothing, and tools for goods such as tobacco and wampum beads. Wampum was especially treasured. The Iroquois wove the beads, made from polished shells, into belts whose patterns might commemorate important events or great deeds. The belts were given as gifts to celebrate a marriage or to ease a mourner's grief after the death of a loved one. Hodenosaunee traders ventured hundreds of miles on foot in search of wampum and other valuables. To travel quickly along lakes and rivers, they used sturdy canoes made from wood and bark. The biggest canoes could carry as many as twenty traders, hunters, or warriors.

When Europeans began to arrive in North America, just a few years after Columbus's first voyage, the Iroquois welcomed them as new trading partners. The French, Dutch, and British brought copper kettles, iron axes, cloth, and other items that the Iroquois were happy to swap for animal furs. Both sides thought they were getting a bargain. Beaver felt hats and warm mink coats were in such demand in Europe that fur traders could make a fortune from a single shipload. The Hodenosaunee found the Europeans' cloth easier to sew than animal skins and their metal tools more practical than native tools of stone or wood.

Because of their powerful confederacy, the Iroquois people at first did not fear the foreigners. In time, though, the fur trade would threaten their way of life. Foreign traders brought diseases such as smallpox and measles, which were new to the continent and killed thousands of Native Americans. And when France and Great Britain competed with one another for control of North America, the People of the Longhouse were drawn into those conflicts. By the time of the American Revolution, the Iroquois had to choose sides. When nearly all of the tribes sided with the British, George Washington took revenge by destroying many of their villages. After the war some of the Iroquois nations moved to Canada and many moved west. The Onondaga and most of the Seneca remained on reservations in New York State.

THE AZTECS
THE GODS COME TO TENOCHTITLÁN

Of all the peoples living in the Americas around 1500, only the Aztecs were expecting foreign visitors. Montezuma II, emperor of the Aztec civilization in what is now Mexico, had been puzzling over heavenly signs that something big was about to happen. First there was a tongue of fire in the sky: a comet that burned brilliantly every night for a year. Then a temple was destroyed by a lightning bolt, but no thunder was heard. Most mysterious of all was the strange bird—like a crane but of an odd ashen color—brought to the imperial palace by a fisherman. When the emperor looked at the bird, he saw a vision of a mirror on its head. In the mirror rows of armed warriors approached, riding on deer. Montezuma called for his priests and counselors, but by the time they arrived, both mirror and vision had vanished.

Were all these unnatural happenings a sign of the gods' displeasure? In the Aztec world there were hundreds of different gods, each governing a particular human activity or part of nature: the sun, the earth, lakes and rivers, hope, healing, games, war. Two centuries earlier, legends said, the gods had led the Aztec people from their barren lands in the north to the fertile Valley of Mexico. The gods promised that the people would recognize their new home when they saw an eagle perched on a cactus, eating a serpent. The Aztecs found the eagle on an island in the middle of a lake, and there they built their magnificent new capital, Tenochtitlán. At the very center of the capital, they built a great pyramid temple, nine stories high. Human sacrifices were made at the Great Temple to please the gods, who needed blood to remain strong. In a dramatic and terrible ceremony, the heart of the victim was cut from the chest and the blood

Craftspeople make and sell their wares in the busy open-air marketplace in Tenochtitlán. The Aztec capital was built on an island on the site of present-day Mexico City.

The Aztecs often practiced human and animal sacrifice. They considered the blood of a warrior to be the offering most pleasing to the gods. This record of a sacrifice of prisoners of war comes from an Aztec codex—a kind of picture writing on paper or animal hide.

was sprinkled like holy water over the temple walls and steps.

Most sacrificial victims were captured enemy soldiers. Through wars of conquest the Aztec emperors had extended their reach far beyond the Valley of Mexico, building an empire that stretched 125,000 square miles, from the Pacific Ocean in the west to the Gulf of Mexico in the east. Montezuma did more than any other emperor to expand the Aztec Empire—and to honor the Aztec gods. After one particularly rewarding campaign, he is said to have had 12,000 enemy soldiers sacrificed at once.

Such a vast and powerful empire seemed safe from threats from the outside world. But Montezuma couldn't stop thinking about those heavenly signs. In the spring of 1518, the mystery deepened. A laborer arrived at the

The Aztecs dyed feathers with bright colors for use
as ornaments in clothing, costumes, and headdresses.

imperial court with news of "some big hills, floating in the sea." The
emperor sent an adviser to the coast to investigate. When the Aztec
climbed a tree and peered out over the water, he saw men rowing to land
in small fishing boats, then returning to the objects in the sea. Quickly
he carried his report back to the emperor: the "hills" were actually huge
ships filled with men.

The foreigners sailed away, but a year later their big ships returned.
Led by Spanish explorer Hernán Cortés, five hundred soldiers and sixteen
horses landed on the coast of Mexico, near the modern port of Veracruz.
The men were conquistadores—Spanish conquerors. Since Columbus's
first voyage to the New World in 1492, Spain had been busy setting up
colonies and trading posts in Cuba, the West Indies, and Central America.
Cortés and his men were part of the next wave of "exploration." Bearing
swords, crossbows, muskets, and cannons, they had come not to discover and
trade but to conquer new lands for Spain and new converts for Christianity.

Montezuma shook with dread when he heard of the foreigners' arrival.
The strangers were odd looking: white skin, long black or red beards,
shining armor. The "deer" they rode were said to be "high as rooftops,"
and their deafening cannons could tear a tree to splinters. Could they be
gods? Could their leader be Quetzalcoatl, the great god of learning, hope,
and healing? Quetzalcoatl, who was believed to have lived with the Aztecs
in ancient times, was often pictured in old drawings as a bearded man with
a white face. Legends said that long ago, in the year 1-Reed of the Aztec
calendar, Quetzalcoatl had sailed away on a raft of serpents into the sun
rising in the east. It was the year 1-Reed again, and the godlike strangers
had come from the east. Montezuma decided it would be wise to be friendly
to the visitors, just in case. Hoping to bribe them into staying away from
his capital city, the emperor sent messengers bearing baskets piled high
with treasure: jewelry, bells, shields, masks, headdresses, fans, and more—
all made of gold and brilliant green feathers.

The Spaniards pawed eagerly through Montezuma's gifts. Then, more determined than ever to claim their prize, Cortés and his men set out for Tenochtitlán. It took three months of hard marching—harder than necessary, thanks to Aztec guides who deliberately led them along the most difficult paths—but the conquistadores finally reached the glittering Aztec capital.

Out came Montezuma, riding on a fine litter carried by his noblemen. Splendid in an embroidered cloak, green feathered headdress, and sandals studded with precious gems, the Aztec emperor greeted the steel-clad Cortés and invited him into the city. But it soon became obvious that the Spaniards were no gods. They behaved abominably, looting the temples, stealing the emperor's crown and royal robes, even taking the emperor himself prisoner. When the conquistadores attacked and murdered a group of worshippers at a religious festival, the Aztecs fought back. Spears, arrows, and stones battled steel swords and crossbows. Blood ran like water in the city streets. Montezuma himself was killed. After many days of fierce fighting, the Spanish were forced to flee the city.

A year later Cortés returned. This time he brought thousands of soldiers, sailing in ships equipped with cannons to bombard Tenochtitlán. The siege lasted eighty days. Trapped in their island city, with the smoke from the burning buildings and gunfire blotting out the sky, the Aztecs slowly starved. At last the victorious

Cortés and Montezuma meet outside Tenochtitlán. Standing next to Cortés is Marina, an Aztec woman who was taken captive by the Spaniards and served as their guide and interpreter.

THE AZTEC CALENDARS

The Aztecs ordered their days according to two calendars: one for everyday life and a sacred calendar for the priests. The everyday calendar, the *xihuitl*, had 365 days, divided into eighteen months, with 5 "extra" days tacked on at the end of the year. This calendar was used to keep track of religious ceremonies and festivals. It also told farmers the proper time to plant and harvest each of their crops. The priests' calendar, the *Tehalpohualli*, had only 260 days, grouped into twenty months of 13 days each. Every day had a different name and a different god associated with it. Priests used this sacred calendar to predict the fortunes of every Aztec child, according to the day of the child's birth. A child was lucky to be born on 4-Dog, but only misfortune awaited the boy or girl born on 9-Wind. The calendar also predicted lucky days for new ventures, such as starting a journey or going to war.

The names of Aztec years in the everyday calendar were a combination of numbers (from 1 through 13) and signs (Reed, Flint, House, and Rabbit). The year Cortés entered Tenochtitlan, 1519, was 1-Reed to the Aztecs. The year of the Spanish conquest, 1521, was 3-House.

Once every fifty-two years, both of the Aztecs' calendars came together, so that the first day of the *xihuitl* and the first day of the *Tehalpohualli* were the same. The "tying of the years" was the beginning of a new century. On this sacred and somewhat scary occasion, the Aztecs carried new fire to their temples and gave thanks that the world had not come to an end.

Spaniards marched into the ruins of the battered capital.

Cortés had conquered an empire. Nearly a half million Aztecs had been killed in the fighting, and many more would die in the days ahead from diseases brought by the foreigners. Atop the rubble of the once-magnificent

This circular stone sculpture may have been an ancient Aztec calendar.

Aztec capital rose Christian churches and homes for the Spanish settlers who flocked to the land that Cortés renamed New Spain. And the treasures of Tenochtitlán's temples were stolen, destroyed, or buried beneath the ruins, for archaeologists to discover centuries later.

THE INCAS
ATAHUALLPA FILLS A ROOM WITH GOLD

In 1493, while Europe buzzed with the news of Columbus's voyage to the New World, Huayna Capac took the throne in western South America. Huayna Capac was the Sapa Inca, or semidivine ruler of the Inca Empire, the richest and most powerful empire in the Americas. The Inca Empire stretched more than two thousand miles north to south and two hundred miles east to west. Its lands make up modern-day Peru and parts of Chile, Argentina, Bolivia, Ecuador, and Colombia. Some 200,000 people lived in Cuzco, the Inca capital. Cuzco was a beautiful city of fine stone palaces and temples with walls coated with silver and gold.

The Sapa Inca did much to increase the power and grandeur of his empire. He led his army on long campaigns of war in the north, conquering new lands. To ensure the loyalty of his conquered subjects, Huayna Capac left Inca nobles in charge of the local rulers and sent the rulers' children to school in Cuzco. That discouraged the parents from making trouble and created a whole new generation of loyal Incas.

To keep in touch with his ever-growing empire, Huayna Capac expanded on a system of roads that had been started by earlier emperors. Two paved highways stretched north and south for thousands of miles, one along the Pacific coast, the other along the line of the high Andes Mountains. Smaller roads branched off to towns and villages, crossing rivers, deserts, and mountain ridges. Inca engineers carved tunnels through rock, cut steps in steep hillsides, and built sturdy rope bridges over river canyons. Trained runners called *chasquis* carried royal messages quickly along the excellent roads. Every four or five miles there was a stone hut where a *chasqui* was stationed; each runner raced from his station to the next, repeating the

The Incas' fortress city of Machu Picchu stood on a high ridge between two mountain peaks. The ancient city's ruins cover five square miles of skillfully crafted stone buildings and terraces, linked by three thousand stone steps.

FRANCISCO PISARRO

message to a fresh runner, who took it the next leg of the journey. In this way messages could travel as far as 250 miles in a single day.

In 1525 Huayna Capac died without telling anyone which of his two sons, Atahuallpa or Huáscar, should inherit the throne. Civil war broke out between the brothers and their followers. After years of fighting Atahuallpa won the war by capturing Huáscar. In 1532 the new Sapa Inca marched his army triumphantly back toward Cuzco. But the bitter war had divided the Inca Empire, killing thousands of people and leaving many Inca cities in ruins. Just at that moment—when the empire was at its weakest—a deadly new threat appeared on the horizon.

Francisco Pizarro, like many of Spain's conquistadores, had been inspired by Cortés's conquest of the Aztecs. Pizarro wanted his own rich empire to conquer. He persuaded Spain's King Charles I (grandson of Ferdinand and Isabella) to fund a small expedition. In 1532, after a long and difficult voyage down the west coast of South America, Pizarro and his army of 168 invaders marched into Peru.

Hearing reports of the foreigners in his land, Atahuallpa sent a messenger, inviting the Spaniards to visit his army's camp, near the town of Cajamarca. Pizarro saw his chance to mount an ambush. The Spanish leader hid his soldiers in the buildings that surrounded the town's enclosed central square. From their hiding places the conquistadores watched as the Sapa Inca's servants approached, sweeping the ground with long straws. Next came six thousand unarmed Inca soldiers, priests, and courtiers. Finally Atahuallpa, wearing a gold crown and a collar of massive emeralds, arrived, carried into the square on a litter lined with bright parrot feathers. Pizarro sent a priest forward with a cross and Bible. According to one version of the encounter, when the priest told the Sapa Inca that the Bible contained the

Francisco Pizarro, the Spanish conquistador who conquered the Inca Empire, was known for his courage, cunning, greed, and ambition.

STONE VERSUS GUNPOWDER

The Chinese people invented gunpowder, an explosive mixture of potassium nitrate, charcoal, and sulfur, around A.D. 800. When traders brought this powder west, Europeans came up with the idea of using it to launch stone projectiles from barrel-like tubes made of oak and hooped with iron. These early cannons first appeared in the 1300s. Heavy and awkward to move, they were only practical during a long siege of a town. Soon cannons made of iron and mounted on wheels began to appear, and Europeans also learned to use gunpowder in a heavy but portable musket.

Warriors in the New World had no firearms. They wielded sling-shots, bows and arrows, and clubs, knives, and spears tipped with stone or bronze. Such weapons proved ineffective against the overwhelming power of the firearms—as well as the crossbows and steel swords—carried by European soldiers.

The invaders' horses filled the Incas with awe. The people of the Americas had never seen a horse before, and they found the fast, powerful, trampling beasts terrifying. A nephew of the Inca emperor Atahuallpa said that the Spaniards seemed like gods to his people, because they "rode on enormous animals that had feet of silver" and carried muskets firing "thunder from heaven."

words of the one true God, Atahuallpa held the book to his ear and then, when no words came out, threw it to the ground in disgust. The enraged priest ran from the square, shouting, "Come out Christians! Come at these enemy dogs who reject the things of God." At a signal

This gold animal head is one of the few remaining examples of Inca artistry. The conquistadores, interested only in the precious metals from which the Inca treasures were made, melted them down into gold and silver bars.

CONQVISTA
CORTÁLE·LA·CAVESA·A
ATAGVALDA·INGA·VMATACVCHV

murio atagualpa
conla ciudad de caxamarca

geronimo

from their leader, the conquistadores sprang from hiding, charging their horses and swinging their long steel swords. Trapped by the surrounding walls, terrified by the trampling horses, thousands of Incas were slaughtered, and the Sapa Inca was captured.

Observing that the Spaniards were fascinated with gold and silver, the Sapa Inca offered to fill a room with treasure in return for his freedom. Pizarro readily agreed. For the next seven months, Atahuallpa's subjects carted in beautifully crafted jars, pitchers, vases, masks, statues, jewelry, plates, spoons—even the royal throne. The Spaniards melted down all these artistic treasures into gold and silver bars. Then Pizarro divided the ransom among his men, saving the lion's share for himself and the Spanish king. Finally, fearing that the Sapa Inca's followers might try to rescue him and stage a rebellion, the Spaniards sentenced Atahuallpa to death. The Inca ruler was baptized as a Christian and then put to death.

Atahuallpa's followers were stunned and disheartened by their leader's execution. Already weakened by years of war, the mighty Inca Empire fell to Spain. Conquistadores entered Cuzco and the empire's other major towns and cities, taking over the gold mines, fortresses, temples, and storehouses. Men from Peru's villages were forced to work in the Spanish-run mines and many died. Rebellions flared up from time to time but were squashed quickly and brutally. In 1572 the last nationwide rebellion failed.

What about Francisco Pizarro and his fellow conquistadores? Soon after the conquest they began fighting among themselves over the division of Inca territory. In 1541 Pizarro was murdered by one of his rivals. Some said that the ghost of Atahuallpa had taken its final revenge.

The execution of Atahuallpa. The Spanish artist who made this woodcut put a cross in the Inca ruler's hands as a sign of his baptism as a Christian.

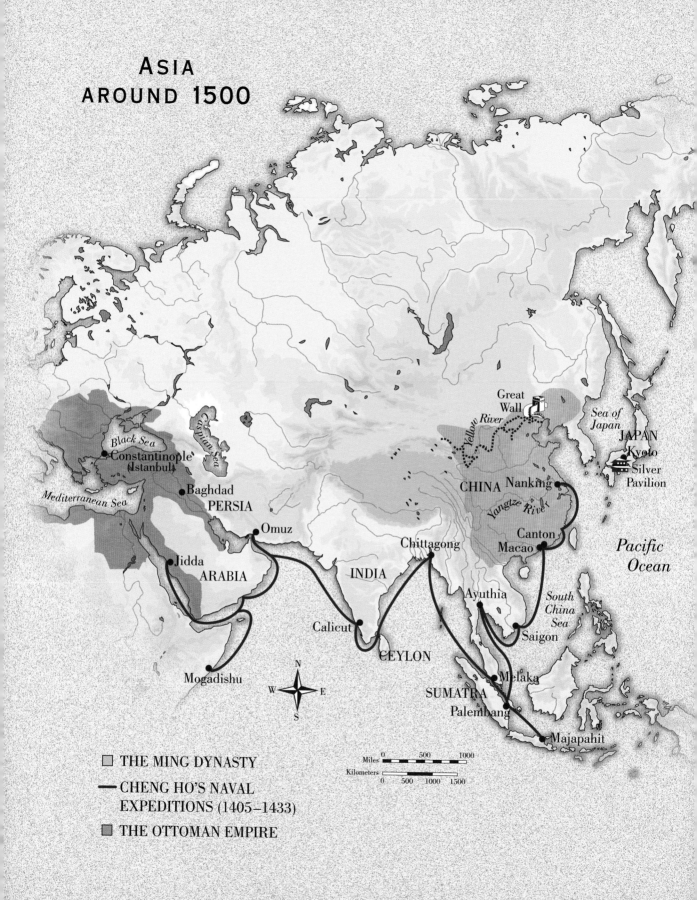

ASIA
AROUND 1500

Black Sea
Constantinople
(Istanbul)

Mediterranean Sea

Caspian Sea

Baghdad
PERSIA

Omuz

Jidda
ARABIA

Mogadishu

INDIA

Calicut

CEYLON

Chittagong

Great
Wall

Yellow River

CHINA Nanking

Yangtze River

Canton
Macao

Sea of Japan

JAPAN
Kyoto
Silver
Pavilion

Pacific Ocean

Ayuthia

South China Sea

Saigon

Melaka

SUMATRA
Palembang

Majapahit

N
W   E
S

THE MING DYNASTY

CHENG HO'S NAVAL
EXPEDITIONS (1405–1433)

THE OTTOMAN EMPIRE

Miles 0   500   1000
Kilometers
0   500   1000   1500

PART III

ASIA

Five hundred years ago, Asia—the land explorers had been seeking when they stumbled across the Americas— remained largely free of European influence. Around 1500 the Ming dynasty was in power in China. Japan was under the rule of the Ashikaga shoguns with their famous samurai warriors. Japan was struggling, however, with the effects of a bitter civil war. And China faced the threat of invasion along its northern borders. Meanwhile, across the continent in the west, the Ottoman Turks were expanding their empire, determined to spread the faith of Islam.

WHEN THEY RULED

The Ottoman Empire
c. 1300–1924

In China, The Ming Dynasty
1368–1644

In Japan, The Ashikaga Dynasty
1338–1573

THE OTTOMANS

THE SULTANS SPREAD ISLAM

Twenty-year-old Mehmed II, sultan of the Ottoman Empire, gazed at the walls of Constantinople. For seven days the sultan's huge cannons—capable of hurling a quarter-ton cannonball more than a mile—had been bombarding the city's three massive walls. Now the outer wall lay in ruins. The gaping holes were patched with wooden barriers slapped together by the city's defenders. Mehmed decided that it was time to send in his army of 100,000 warriors.

Constantinople's 7,000 defenders fought back bravely. Again and again they withstood assaults by Ottoman foot soldiers and blasts from the sultan's ships in the surrounding seas. But after fifty-four days the city could not hold out any longer. Just before dawn on May 29, 1453, the attackers swarmed through a hole in the city's outer wall, broke open a gate, and flooded into Constantinople. They plundered homes and churches; slaughtered thousands of men, women, and children; and took thousands more prisoner, to be sold into slavery. As his men exulted, the sultan rode his horse through the streets to the city's great cathedral. There he picked up a handful of earth and poured it over his head as a sign of humility before God. Then Mehmed converted the church into a Muslim house of worship, at the same time renaming the city. "Hereafter my capital is Istanbul," he proclaimed.

By the mid-1400s the Ottomans had carved out an empire that included much of Asia Minor (the western peninsula in modern-day Turkey) and large areas of southeastern Europe, stretching as far as the Danube River. The Ottomans originally came from central Asia. Because they were a Turkish-speaking people, they came to be called Turks or Ottoman Turks.

The Ottoman Turks built their empire largely through the conquest of

This portrait of Mehmed II by a fifteenth-century Islamic artist emphasizes the warlike sultan's devotion to beauty and the arts. Today Mehmed (also known as Muhammad the Conqueror) is considered the true founder of the Ottoman Empire.

territories belonging to the once-mighty Byzantine Empire. The Byzantines were Christians, and their capital at Constantinople was the center of the Christian Eastern Orthodox Church. Located across a narrow waterway from the tip of Asia Minor, between the Black and Aegean Seas, Constantinople guarded the mainland trade routes between Europe and Asia. Over the centuries armies from the world's great kingdoms had attacked Constantinople dozens of times, succeeding in scaling its high walls only once. Many people believed that the glorious Byzantine capital could never be taken.

They underestimated the power of Mehmed. Patient, ambitious, and sometimes cruel, the young sultan inherited the Ottoman throne in 1451. To prevent future challenges to his rule, Mehmed immediately had his infant half brother smothered. Nothing would stand in the way of his goal. Since childhood Mehmed had been convinced that he was destined to rule a great empire. The capital of that empire would be Constantinople, center of Christianity. To Mehmed, the world could have only one empire, one ruler, and one faith: Islam.

The Ottomans were Muslims, or followers of Islam. The religion of Islam is based on the teachings of the prophet Muhammad, who lived in Arabia in the late sixth and early seventh centuries A.D. Muslims believe that there is only one God, Allah. Their holy book, the Koran, is said to contain the words of Allah as revealed to Muhammad. As the Prophet instructed, Muslims build their lives around a strict pattern of prayers, fasts, feasts, and pilgrimages. The Ottoman sultans believed that it was their duty to spread the Muslim faith across the world. Just as the Spanish who conquered the New World acted in the name of the Christian God, the Muslims of the Ottoman Empire dedicated their conquests to the glory of Allah.

To the Christians of western Europe, Constantinople's fall was a dark and dreadful disaster. The Church had been violated by a man many called the "prince of the army of Satan." On a more practical level, the closing of the last trade route to Asia squeezed the pockets of European traders and

A Turkish artist's view of Istanbul around 1500.

merchants. In time that economic crisis would send Columbus and other
European explorers on their voyages in search of sea routes to the Indies.

But Constantinople itself—the city Mehmed renamed Istanbul—flourished
under the Ottomans. The sultan ordered the city's old buildings restored

Suleiman the Magnificent ruled the Ottoman Empire at the height of its power and splendor. Here the sultan accepts the surrender of Belgrade, in present-day Serbia.

and built many beautiful new schools and mosques, as well as a magnificent palace ornamented with gold, silver, and precious gems. He planted wondrous gardens filled with rare plants and birds, and he assembled a huge library of books on science, geography, economy, and religion. Despite his devotion to Islam, Mehmed allowed people of many different faiths and nationalities— Christians, Jews, Greeks, Armenians, Italians, Serbians—to live and work in the city. Non-Muslims were allowed to practice their faith as long as they paid a tribute, in money or military service, to the sultan. At one time Istanbul was home to people from more than seventy different nationalities, making it the only truly international capital in Europe.

After Mehmed's death in 1481, other sultans continued to expand the Ottoman Turks' domain. By the time the empire reached its peak of power in the mid-1600s, the soldiers of Islam had conquered land on three continents: Europe, Asia, and Africa. One of the greatest of the Ottoman sultans, Suleiman I, who came to the throne in 1520, swallowed up vast lands in Armenia, Croatia, Persia (modern-day Iran), and Hungary. Known as Suleiman the Magnificent, this sultan inspired a golden age in which literature, science, education, art, and crafts such as carpet weaving and tile making flourished. In an inscription carved in 1538, Suleiman summed up the ambition and religious devotion that inspired all Ottoman sultans:

I am God's slave and sultan of this world. By the grace of God I am head of Muhammad's community. God's might and Muhammad's miracles are my companions.... In Baghdad I am the shah, in Byzantine realms the Caesar, and in Egypt the sultan, who sends his fleets to the seas of Europe, Maghrib [Africa], and India.

THE CHINESE
CHENG HO RULES THE EASTERN SEAS

Decades before Europeans explored Africa, Admiral Cheng Ho (sometimes called Zheng-he) was carrying African treasures home to his emperor in China. Cheng Ho's specially constructed ships were large—some more than four hundred feet long. On his first voyage, in 1405, he sailed with a fleet of sixty-three ships and nearly 28,000 sailors, soldiers, and traders. The admiral's seven grand expeditions took him to the islands of the South China Sea and on to the Indian Ocean, to India, Ceylon (Sri Lanka), Persia (Iran), Arabia, and down the east coast of Africa. No other nation had ever ventured so far from its home waters.

The man who sponsored Cheng Ho's voyages was Yung-lo, second emperor of the Ming dynasty, which ruled China from 1368 to 1644. The Ming emperors had come to the throne by expelling the Mongols, Asian conquerors who had ruled China for many years. Yung-lo was eager to show off the might and glory of his triumphant dynasty—and to grow richer and more powerful. He sent his admiral out to extend China's reach across the seas. As Cheng Ho explored foreign lands, he set up trading posts in ports such as Melaka, a city in Malaysia. At the same time, with his great ships and thousands of people, he impressed foreign rulers with the might of the Ming emperor. Everywhere he landed, Cheng Ho demanded tribute. Most kings quickly agreed. It couldn't hurt to make friends with such a powerful ruler, and besides, the admiral gave his own rich gifts in return. Rulers of more than twenty different kingdoms filled Cheng Ho's treasure ships with lavish gifts. The Chinese brought back cargoes laden with pearls, spices, rich woods, and exotic plants and animals, including zebras, ostriches, and one lone giraffe. The few kings who were less cooperative suffered the

A Chinese naval ship prepares to battle Japanese pirates. This detail from a narrative scroll—a painting made on a long roll of paper that tells a story as it is unrolled—was created during the early Ming dynasty.

consequences. Cheng Ho dethroned several foreign rulers, replacing them with monarchs more to his liking. Sometimes he brought troublesome kings back to China, to explain their behavior to the emperor personally. It was also said that, on the Indonesian island of Sumatra, the admiral had five thousand people massacred when their ruler failed to make the proper payments.

After Yung-lo's death in 1424, the Chinese began to withdraw from the outside world. Many members of the imperial court were concerned that contact with foreigners—people they considered barbarians—would pollute

THE GREAT WALL OF CHINA

The world's longest monument got its start as many separate piles of earth. As far back as 1500 B.C., the Chinese people were building earthen walls around their cities for protection from neighboring Chinese states and outside invaders. In the early third century B.C., Qin Shi-huangdi (cheen-shr-hwahng-dee), the emperor who united China, began the long and difficult process of linking all the walls along the country's northern border. Tribes from the north often swooped down on horseback to raid China's fertile farmland, and Emperor Qin planned to keep them out. During his reign, nearly a million laborers worked on the project. They built long connecting walls of earth, clay bricks, and stone, with thousands of tall watchtowers and outposts for soldiers. So many people died building the 1,800-mile-long barrier that the Great Wall has been called "the longest cemetery on earth."

Later emperors sometimes expanded the Great Wall, sometimes neglected it. By the time the Ming dynasty came to power in 1368, the wall had grown to 3,000 miles but many sections lay in ruins. Mongol invaders from the north had hacked out gaping holes, and weeds popped up among the stones. The Ming emperors spent two hundred years repairing the damage. They restored and lengthened the wall and added a top layer of solid brick, crowned by strong defense towers. By

China's superior culture. There were also other, more urgent dangers. Japanese pirates had begun to roam the eastern seas, attacking Chinese vessels. Horsemen from the Mongol lands to the north were again raiding Chinese border towns, and the Great Wall, built centuries earlier to keep out invaders,

The Great Wall of China is the longest structure ever built by hand. During the time of the Ming emperors, it stretched 3,000 miles. This section, near the modern capital city of Beijing, has been restored as an attraction for tourists.

1500 the Great Wall snaked like a magnificent dragon for thousands of miles along the curves and dips of China's many mountain chains. To a Portuguese visitor in the 1550s, it was an awe-inspiring sight, "a wall of wondrous strength, of a month's journey in extent."

was falling apart. The Ming emperors put their energies into rebuilding the wall and equipping it with well-armed troops. They decided that the best way to protect their kingdom was to remain apart from other nations.

Admiral Cheng Ho's final expedition, in 1433, was also China's last long-

*Founded in 1557, the Portuguese colony of Macao sat
on a rocky peninsula connected to China by a long, narrow
strip of land. For three hundred years, the isolated
settlement was China's only link to the outside world.*

distance voyage for centuries. The Ming emperors outlawed sea travel.
Soon even the building of seagoing ships was prohibited. By the time the
Portuguese began exploring and colonizing the African coast in the late

1400s, Cheng Ho's great fleet was a thing of the past. And when the first Portuguese traders arrived in China soon after 1500, they were treated with contempt and mistrust.

The emperors did make a few compromises. They had always tolerated contact with Muslim traders, for example. And in 1557 they allowed the Portuguese to build a single trading post, Macao, on an uninhabited peninsula at Canton. For centuries all contact with Europeans was funneled through that port. To most Westerners, China remained a distant and mysterious place—a land of silk, spices, and untold riches—until well into the nineteenth century.

The voyages of Cheng Ho were largely forgotten until modern times, when journals kept by two of his captains were rediscovered. But among the Chinese in Melaka and the other trading posts the admiral established along the shores of the Indian Ocean, he was never forgotten. There people still honor Cheng Ho as the founder of their communities and the daring hero of their ancestors.

THE JAPANESE
A SHOGUN PERFECTS THE TEA CEREMONY

Ashikaga Yoshimasa admired the flower arrangement in the tearoom of the Silver Pavilion in Japan. He added a wildflower, ignoring the surprise of his servants. About fifty years old in 1484, Yoshimasa was an important Japanese nobleman. He was expected to surround himself with flowers from his splendid gardens and to let his servants arrange them. After all, Yoshimasa had been a shogun—military leader of all Japan.

An emperor sat on the throne of Japan, but he had no real power. The shoguns, with their loyal armies of samurai warriors, had long been the true rulers of Japan. Yoshimasa was the eighth in a line of shoguns from the Ashikaga family, who has been governing Japan nearly one hundred and fifty years. The Ashikaga shoguns had difficulty controlling the

A samurai warrior cleans his sword after battle. Fierce fighters and master swordsmen, the samurai dominated Japanese government and society for centuries.

***During the rule of the Ashikaga shoguns, samurai
fought battle after battle in Japan's long civil war.***

country. Under their rule Japan's wealthy landowners fought among themselves
for property and power, and peasant riots tore apart the cities and villages.

Yoshimasa knew that he had been responsible for the last terrible civil
war. In 1465, weary of the constant fighting, he had decided to retire. Since
he had no son, he named his younger brother as his heir. But before his
brother could take over the government, Yoshimasa's wife gave birth to a
son. She claimed that the boy was the rightful heir. Japan's samurai warlords quickly divided into two rival camps—one for the brother, one for
the son—and fierce fighting erupted. The Onin War raged for ten years,

THE TEA CEREMONY

Let us then construct a small room in a bamboo grove or under trees, arrange streams and rocks and plant trees and bushes....In this room we can enjoy the streams and rocks as we do the rivers and mountains in Nature....We listen quietly to the boiling water in the kettle, which sounds like a breeze passing through the pine needles, and become oblivious of all worldly woes and worries; we then pour out a dipperful of water from the kettle...and our mental dust is wiped off.

This description of the Japanese tea ceremony was written in the early 1600s by a Zen master of the art. The custom of drinking tea as part of a religious ceremony had been introduced to Japan some four centuries earlier by Chinese Buddhist monks. Under Ashikaga Yoshimasa it spread all across the country, becoming a highly valued form of Zen-inspired art.

The tea ceremony was held in a teahouse—a simply decorated building set in a garden. Elaborate rules governed every step of the ceremony, which could last as long as four hours. There was a proper way for the host to prepare and serve the tea, for guests to enter the teahouse, to sit and speak, to hold their cups. Through these carefully controlled rituals and the elegance of their surroundings, both host and guests were transported to an inner world of peace and beauty. They experienced a sense of their own harmony with nature—an awareness that was the essence of the tea ceremony and the heart of Zen.

leaving the Ashikaga capital at Kyoto in ruins. When it ended in 1477, there was no clear victor. Most of the warlords simply gave up the fight, exhausted...or dead.

In the midst of the Onin War, Yoshimasa carried out his plan to withdraw from the political world, handing the reins of government to his eight-year-old son and the boy's supporters. The former shogun longed for inner peace—something he would never find while surrounded by ambition and violence. In retirement he became a great patron of the arts. Like Lorenzo de' Medici in Florence, Yoshimasa used his wealth and influence to encourage the development of painting and architecture, along with other Japanese arts.

The center of this artistic outpouring was the Silver Pavilion. Yoshimasa built his palace outside Kyoto, on the ruins of a temple destroyed in the Onin War. He ran out of funds before he could cover the walls with silver as planned, so the palace remained black—but the name stuck anyway. The Silver Pavilion was designed as a private world of peace and beauty, with rooms for rest and meditation, all overlooking a miniature lake and landscaped gardens. On the grounds Yoshimasa built Japan's first tearoom. There, among the delicate flower arrangements, hanging scrolls, and sliding rice-paper screens, he introduced his guests to the tea ceremony. Not only high officials and noblemen but samurai warriors, merchants, and other commoners all across Japan were soon practicing the rituals of this quiet, peaceful form of art.

Yoshimasa encouraged artists at the Silver Pavilion to experiment with the new style of painting called *sumi-e*. Using delicate brushstrokes, *sumi-e* artists painted simple, expressive landscapes entirely in black ink. The Ashikaga patron also sponsored the work of Noh performers. In the Noh form of drama, actors wearing colorful masks and costumes performed slow, graceful dance steps, accompanied by the music of a flute and drums. A chanting chorus helped the actors tell the story of a hero from samurai legend or ghosts and demons from the spirit world.

Noh drama, *sumi-e* painting, the tea ceremony, and other forms of art sponsored by Yoshimasa were all inspired by Zen Buddhism. Since the sixth century many Japanese had followed the religion of Buddhism, but the form known as Zen only became popular in the fourteenth century, when it was adopted by the samurai. Zen Buddhism emphasized simplicity, self-reliance, and self-understanding. Followers looked for inner peace through meditation, sitting cross-legged and motionless for hours, with their minds clear of thoughts and desires, open to enlightenment.

Ashikaga Yoshimasa was a profound believer in Zen Buddhism, and he encouraged art that reflected the simplicity and discipline of Zen. At the Silver Pavilion's beautiful ponds and gardens, guests might spend hours

Noh plays were performed on a bare stage by actors wearing elaborate masks and costumes. A chanting chorus (on the left) helped explain the action.

Yoshimasa's Silver Pavilion was built facing east, away from the miseries suffered by the Japanese people during the Age of the Country at War.

meditating on the moon reflected in the water or the message hidden in the arrangements of pebbles and sand. Noh performers and *sumi-e* painters used their Zen-inspired self-discipline and inner balance to create beautiful pictures—the actors with their movements, the painters with skilled strokes of the brush. Above all, the tea ceremony was a shining example of Zen self-control and tranquillity. Mastering the strict rituals involved in the ceremony took the dedication of a true Zen scholar.

Despite his love of peace and beauty, Ashikaga Yoshimasa was unable to end the bloodshed in his land. The Onin War was just the first of many wars—so many that the years from 1467 to 1568 in Japan are known as the Age of the Country at War. Soon after that period ended, so did the rule of the Ashikagas. Today these shoguns—especially Yoshimasa—are remembered as weak rulers but great patrons of the arts, responsible for some of Japan's most glorious and lasting cultural achievements.

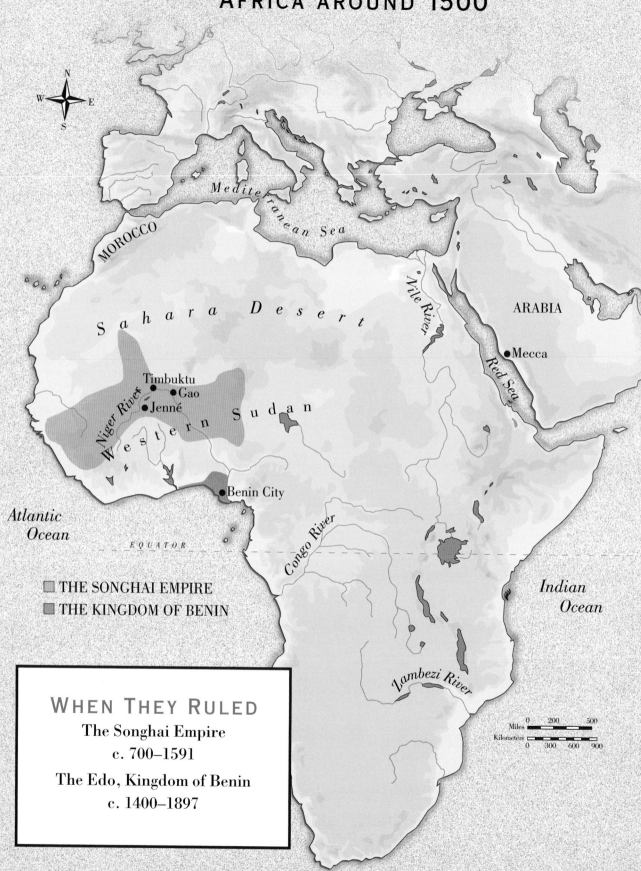

AFRICA AROUND 1500

N W E S (compass rose)

MOROCCO

Mediterranean Sea

Sahara Desert

Nile River

ARABIA

• Mecca

Red Sea

Timbuktu
• Gao
Niger River • Jenné

Western Sudan

• Benin City

Atlantic Ocean

EQUATOR

Congo River

Indian Ocean

Zambezi River

☐ THE SONGHAI EMPIRE
☐ THE KINGDOM OF BENIN

WHEN THEY RULED

The Songhai Empire
c. 700–1591

The Edo, Kingdom of Benin
c. 1400–1897

Miles 0 200 500
Kilometers 0 300 600 900

PART IV

AFRICA

Five hundred years ago, Africa was a land of great contrasts. Many cultures thrived on this vast continent, each with its own unique way of life. Some of the differences among these cultures can be traced to geography. Tropical rain forests, grassy savannas, mountains, swamps, fertile river valleys, barren deserts—people developed different ways of life depending on where they lived. Other contrasts among the peoples of Africa in 1500 came from contacts with the outside world. North and East Africa traded with the Muslims of Arabia, adopting the beliefs and customs of Islam. Meanwhile, along the east and west coasts, Portuguese explorers and missionaries were moving in, eager to seize the riches of the continent and claim its souls for Christianity.

THE SONGHAI
A BALANCING ACT

In North Africa there is a wide belt of grasslands just south of the Sahara Desert, known as the Sudan. Through the ages several empires have risen and fallen in the western part of that region, building their wealth through trade. The largest and most powerful of these was the Songhai. In 1500, at the height of its fame and glory, that empire stretched some two thousand miles along the Niger River, from present-day Senegal to Niger. The kingdom was so large that its soldiers could not patrol its outer reaches and so wealthy that visitors wrote of "treasure inexpressible" and called the Niger a "river of gold."

The leader who built this impressive empire was Sunni Ali. A military captain and fierce warlord, Sunni Ali became king of the Songhai people in 1464. At that time the Songhai were a small nation of traders and merchants. Their principal city was Gao, situated at the southern end of an important caravan route to North Africa. Sunni Ali made up his mind to expand his kingdom. A tireless leader, he spent his days in the saddle, at the head of an army that conquered one neighboring land after another. In 1468 he brought the wealthy city of Timbuktu under his control. Next he laid siege to Jenné, capturing that northern center of trade in gold, kola nuts, and other goods from southern Africa. In the thirty-five years of his reign, the courageous captain was never once defeated.

But Sunni Ali was more than a warlord and conqueror. He was also a wise, farsighted ruler. To control his growing empire, he set up highly organized systems of government. The land was divided into provinces managed by governors and other appointed officials. Everyone in the kingdom had a specific duty: fishermen to supply a certain amount of

Muslim traders, traveling in large camel caravans, risked thirst and deadly sandstorms to cross the deserts of the northern Sudan. These travelers on their way to the rich trading center at Gao were fortunate to find one of the desert's scattered water holes.

The Songhai Empire's Muslim rulers built mosques all across the Sudan. The houses of worship were usually made of mud, which workers constantly renewed by climbing up the wooden posts projecting from the buildings' walls.

dried fish to the king each year, metalworkers to supply spears and arrows, others to provide a variety of different goods and services, such as working in the government or serving in the army. The Songhai king also set up irrigation projects that turned large areas of dry earth into fertile farmland.

To carry out his ambitious programs, Sunni Ali had to perform a tricky balancing act. Early in the eleventh century, the Songhai kings had converted to Islam. Their acceptance of that faith was a big advantage in their many dealings with Muslim traders. Most of the merchants and prominent families of the Songhai cities and market towns also became Muslims. But in the countryside the peasants, who had little or no contact with the empire's trading partners, kept their traditional beliefs. They worshipped a multitude of gods, each believed to hold power over a different aspect of the world: trees, rivers, mountains, snakes, iron, thunder, knowledge. At small temples and shrines presided over by highly respected village priests, the Songhai prayed to their gods for guidance and protection.

The traditional Songhai beliefs and the Muslim faith, with its embrace of one God, were worlds apart. Sunni Ali was a Muslim, as were many of the leaders of his cities and towns. But the Songhai ruler was also a man of the countryside, who had come to power with the support and aid of the villagers. Throughout his rule he tried to balance these opposing ideas. He followed the Muslim practices of prayer and fasts, and he declared his respect for the "learned men" of Islam. At the same time he respected the beliefs and customs of the peasants and the authority of village chiefs over their people.

In 1492, as Columbus sailed to the New World, change was also coming to Songhai. Sunni Ali died, and his son Sunni Baru became king. Sunni Baru sided entirely with the peasants, refusing to accept Islam. After little more than a year, he was forced from the throne by the rebel Askia Muhammad, a strict Muslim. As Songhai's ruler, Askia Muhammad reshaped the empire's laws and customs to bring them more in line with Muslim beliefs and practices. He appointed loyal Muslim officials to his government and gave them more power than the village chiefs. He even made a pilgrimage to Mecca, the holiest city of Islam, where he was named caliph, or deputy ruler, over the western Sudan.

Under the caliph's rule the Songhai Empire soared to new heights. Its army conquered neighboring states to the north, east, and west. Askia Muhammad strengthened the system of government set up by Sunni Ali, making his kingdom even stronger. He invited Muslim scholars to Timbuktu and Jenné, transforming those cities into centers of Islamic culture and education. Around 1500 Leo Africanus, a Muslim traveler from Morocco, described Timbuktu as a splendid city with "many judges, professors and holy men, all being generously helped by the king, who holds scholars in much honor." In that city of learning, Leo Africanus reported, writers published books on history and Islamic law—books in such demand that their sellers made "more profit...than from any other merchandise." The Muslim traveler also described a less attractive form of trade. In the Songhai capital at Gao, he wrote, there was "a market where many slaves, men and women, [were] sold every day" and "little children...sold for about half the price of grown-ups." Slavery was a long-standing tradition in the Sudan. Most slaves were prisoners of war. Though they had few rights or freedoms, slaves in Songhai did have hope: after a few years of forced labor, most were granted their freedom.

The power of the Songhai Empire lasted only a hundred years after Askia Muhammad took power. In 1591 a Muslim army from Morocco crossed the Sahara into Gao and Timbuktu, bearing muskets and cannons acquired through trade with the Portuguese. In the end, it was the Songhai's age-old conflict between Muslims and non-Muslims that proved the empire's downfall. While the peasants battled the invaders, many of the townspeople supported them. The Muslim adviser to the Songhai king betrayed village chiefs to the invading army's leader. And during one key battle, the adviser even persuaded his king to withdraw from the field and abandon Songhai to its conquerors.

Under the Songhai, Timbuktu became a thriving city of nearly 40,000 people. Merchants from northern Africa flocked to this international center of culture and trade to exchange salt, cloth, and other goods for gold and slaves.

THE EDO
LAND OF THE POWERFUL *OBAS*

The crown prince rode through the streets of Benin City on a fine horse trimmed with bells. Before him ran young men blowing on trumpets and chiefs dressed in red robes with brass ornaments. Behind came acrobats leaping and tumbling, musicians playing horns and flutes and drums, hunters leading tame leopards by their chains. Reaching the palace, the prince received the symbolic transfer of the land of Benin from his chiefs. Slaves and leopards were sacrificed in his honor. Then he put on the royal robes of red coral and the pointed coral crown, with its tall spike reaching toward the gods in the heavens. Now he was king and a mere mortal no more, but part man, part god. He held the power of life and death over his people, and the fate of the kingdom was in his hands.

The crowning of Ozolua as *oba*, or semidivine ruler of Benin, took place around 1481. But the details of the ceremony reached back centuries, to the founding of the kingdom by the Edo people sometime in the tenth century A.D. The Edo settled on the west coast of Africa, several hundred miles south of the Songhai Empire, on land that is part of Nigeria today. There, in the forests and fertile Niger River delta, they built a kingdom famous for its riches, its power, and the splendor of its arts.

Unlike the peoples of the western Sudan, most Edo had never seen a Muslim merchant. They followed a religion quite different from Islam, worshipping one supreme god plus many lesser gods and ancestor spirits. At the center of this spiritual world was the *oba*. Through him the gods worked to protect the Edo people. The abundance of crops, victory at war, protection from flood, famine, and disease—all these depended on the mystical powers of the *oba*. Like a god, he never had to wash, eat, or sleep (death to the servant who dared whisper otherwise!). And when the *oba* died, he was buried seated on a throne in a giant grave, along with several living attendants, to take up court in the spirit world.

One of the most famous *obas* was Ewuare the Great, who put on the coral crown around 1440. Ewuare was an energetic, ambitious man. Like Sunni Ali of the Songhai Empire, he led his army far and wide, capturing more than two hundred towns to the north and east and forcing the conquered rulers to pay tribute. As these riches poured in, Ewuare used them to expand his capital

The head of an oba, *or king of Benin, sculpted in brass. The Edo believed that the head was the source of each person's power. The oba's head was considered sacred.*

A HISTORY IN BRASS

The Edo had no written language, but they wanted their history remembered. So the *oba*s ordered skilled artists to create brass relief plaques showing scenes of court life, religious ceremonies, and military victories. Later sculpture showed the coming of the Portuguese, complete with details of the soldiers' long hair, heavy woolen clothing, and guns and crossbows. The art was displayed on large wooden pillars inside the palace. There the *oba*'s "remembrancers" used them to jog their memories when they told stories of the kingdom's past.

Court artists also used their skills to sculpt expressive brass heads of Benin's rulers. To create these sculptures, they used a sophisticated technique known as the lost-wax method. The artist started with a model of the head, made from an eggshell-thin layer of beeswax sandwiched between thick layers of clay. When the mold was heated over a fire, the beeswax melted away, and the sculptor poured the hot liquid metal into the gap where the wax had been. After the brass cooled and hardened, the clay was broken off to reveal the sculpture. The finished head of an *oba* was carried during his funeral ceremonies, then placed in a shrine for future *oba*s to honor.

This brass plaque, showing a warrior chief with his weapons and attendants, decorated the oba's palace. Benin's highly skilled sculptors created hundreds of plaques to record military campaigns and other important events.

The late 1400s brought a new subject for Benin's artists—the first European explorers. This brass image of a helmeted Portuguese soldier carries a matchlock, a kind of musket that uses a slow-burning match to ignite the charge.

at Benin City, building broad streets, a large, splendid palace, and spacious houses with polished red clay walls that shone like marble. Inside the protective walls of Benin City, people lived in separate neighbor-hoods, or wards, according to their jobs: metalworkers in one ward, ivory workers in another, weavers in a third. These craftspeople created magnificent works of art to honor the gods and the *oba*. Ewuare also introduced important political changes, creating a well-organized system of government depart-ments and a council of chiefs and other officials to help him rule.

During Ewuare the Great's reign, Portuguese explorers sailed along the coast of Benin. But it wasn't until 1486, after Ewuare died and Ozolua became *oba*, that the foreigners ventured inland. Led by Portuguese ambas-sador João Affonso d'Aveiro, the visitors traveled to Benin City, where they were greeted by the *oba* in all his glory. Impressed by Ozolua's power, his fearsome army, and the splendor of his capital, the Portuguese quickly abandoned any

*The Portuguese built fortresses along the African coast
to serve as trading posts and supply bases for trading ships.*

thoughts of conquest. But they were eager to trade, and the *oba* was glad to oblige. Soon Portuguese trading ships were shuttling back and forth along the coast, swapping mirrors, glassware, dyed cloth, brass bracelets, iron bars, and cowrie shells for Benin's pepper, cotton cloth, ivory, and slaves. The slaves were mostly prisoners of war and criminals sentenced to unpaid labor for their crimes. At first Benin's *oba*s refused to export young male slaves, who were needed to keep the kingdom strong. But in time they dropped that rule, tempted by the high prices paid for slaves destined for a life of misery in European colonies in the New World.

Trading was profitable for both sides—even though the Portuguese often complained that the Edo drove a hard bargain. "These Africans are very wary people in their bargaining," warned one ship's captain, "and anyone dealing with them must use them gently." The crafty master traders appointed by the *oba* might haggle for days or even weeks to get the price they wanted, sometimes stomping out during negotiations to force the other side to settle. As time passed and other European nations joined the scramble for Africa's treasures, the Edo played one against the other—if the Portuguese wouldn't deal, there were always the British, the French, and the Dutch.

In 1500 clever strategies like these saved the Edo from becoming victims of European domination the way the peoples of the Americas and other African coastal nations had. Instead, the kingdom of Benin thrived well into the late 1800s, when civil wars and the decline of the profitable slave trade weakened it, allowing an invading English army to absorb the once-mighty land of the *oba*s into the British Empire.

WORLD EVENTS AROUND 1500

1405—Chinese admiral Cheng Ho sets sail on his first voyage

1424—Emperor Yun-lo dies, and the Chinese begin to withdraw from the outside world

1433—Admiral Cheng Ho makes his final voyage

c. 1440—Ewuare the Great becomes *oba* of Benin

1451—Mehmed I becomes sultan of the Ottoman Empire

1452—The Ming emperor prohibits sailing in Chinese coastal waters

1453—The Ottoman Turks conquer the Byzantine capital of Constantinople

1462—Ivan III becomes grand duke of Moscow

1464—Sunni Ali becomes king of Gao and begins to build the Songhai Empire

1465—Shogun warrior Ashikaga Yoshimasa decides to give up his leadership of Japan, leading to the
        Onin War

1467–1477—Onin War in Japan

1468—Sunni Ali captures Timbuktu

1471—Ivan conquers Novgorod

1473—Yoshimasa Ashikaga retires as shogun of Japan

1474—Isabella becomes queen of Castile and León

c.1480—Ivan the Great challenges the Mongols, leading to the end of Mongol rule in Russia

c.1481—Ozolua becomes *oba* of Benin

1486—Portuguese ambassador João Affonso d'Aveiro arrives in Benin
        —Christopher Columbus presents his plan for exploration to King Ferdinand and
           Queen Isabella of Spain

1492—Spain defeats the Moors at Granada—Christopher Columbus reaches the New World—Sunni Ali
        dies, and his son Sunni Baru becomes the king of Songhai

1493—Huayna Capac becomes Sapa Inca of the Inca Empire—Askia Muhammad becomes
        ruler of Songhai

c.1500—Portuguese traders arrive in China

1501—Amerigo Vespucci explores the coast of South America, recognizing it as a separate continent

1502—Montezuma II becomes emperor of the Aztec Empire

1503—Leonardo da Vinci completes the *Mona Lisa*

1512—Michelangelo completes the ceiling of the Sistine Chapel in Rome

1513—Juan Ponce de León discovers Florida; Vasco Nuñez reaches the Pacific Ocean

1519—Hernán Cortés lands in Mexico

1520—Suleiman I becomes sultan of the Ottoman Empire

1521—Cortés conquers the Aztec Empire

c.1525—The Iroquois Confederacy is formed

1532—Atahuallpa becomes Sapa Inca of the Inca Empire; Francisco Pizarro conquers the Incas

1557—The Chinese allow the Portuguese to buld a trading post at Macao

GLOSSARY

apothecary Someone who prepares and sells medicines; in Renaissance times apothecaries also sold herbs, spices, sugar, and dyes.

Buddhism The religion based on the fifth-century B.C. teachings of the Indian wise man known as the Buddha, or "Enlightened One"; Buddhism emphasizes rules of ideal behavior and the practice of meditation.

caliph A Muslim leader; one who follows in the footsteps of the prophet Muhammad.

city-state An independent political body consisting of a city and its surrounding lands.

cowrie shells Small oval seashells that were once used as money in some African nations.

dynasty A series of rulers who belong to the same family.

Islam The religious faith of Muslims, who believe that Allah is the one God and Muhammad is his prophet.

kola nuts The reddish brown seeds of the kola tree, which contain caffeine and can be chewed as a stimulant; today kola nuts are mainly used in soft drinks.

longhouse The traditional Iroquois dwelling, made from a frame of saplings covered with tree bark shingles.

medieval Having to do with the Middle Ages, the period of European history from about A.D. 500 to 1450.

mosque A Muslim place of worship.

Noh theater A traditional form of Japanese theater, in which masked actors and a chanting chorus perform plays based on samurai legends or stories from the spirit world.

oba The semidivine ruler of the kingdom of Benin.

pilgrimage A journey made to a shrine or other sacred place.

relief A type of sculpture in which designs are engraved or carved to stand out from a flat surface.

Renaissance The period of European history from about the late four-teenth to mid-seventeenth centuries, marked by tremendous advances in knowledge, literature, science, and the arts.

ritual A series of actions performed in a certain fixed way, usually as part of a ceremony.

samurai A Japanese warrior.

Sapa Inca "Unique or supreme Inca"; a title of the Inca emperor.

shogun One of the military rulers of Japan from the twelfth to mid-nineteenth centuries.

sultan The king of certain Muslim countries.

sumi-e A Japanese art form in which the artist uses delicate brushstrokes and black ink to create landscapes.

tribute Payment to a ruler, made to show respect and submission.

wampum Small purple or white beads made from polished shells, once highly valued by Native American tribes in the Northeast.

Zen Buddhism A form of Buddhism that emphasizes self-discipline and meditation as ways to balance the mind, body, and spirit.

FOR FURTHER READING

Barnes-Svarney, Patricia. *Zimbabwe*. Philadelphia: Chelsea House, 1999.

Bial, Raymond. *The Iroquois*. New York: Marshall Cavendish, 1999.

Brenner, Barbara. *If You Were There in 1492: Everyday Life in the Time of Columbus*. New York: Aladdin, 1998.

Capaldi, Gina. *Africa: Customs, Cultures, Legends, and Lore*. Torrance, CA: Good Apple, 1997.

Chambers, Catherine. *West African States: 15th Century to Colonial Era*. Austin, TX: Raintree Steck-Vaughn, 1999.

Clare, John D., ed. *Italian Renaissance*. San Diego: Harcourt Brace, 1995.

Fritz, Jean. *Around the World in a Hundred Years: From Henry the Navigator to Magellan*. New York: G. P. Putnam, 1994.

Hakim, Joy. *The First Americans*. New York: Oxford University Press, 1993.

Haskins, James, and Kathleen Benson. *African Beginnings*. New York: Morrow, 1998.

James, R. S. *Mozambique*. Philadelphia: Chelsea House, 1999.

Levine, Ellen. *If You Lived with the Iroquois*. New York: Scholastic, 1998.

Mann, Kenny. *African Kingdoms of the Past: Monomotapa, Zulu, Basuto*. Parsippany, NJ: Dillon, 1996.

Martell, Hazel Mary. *The World of Islam before 1700*. Austin, TX: Raintree Steck-Vaughn, 1999.

Mason, Antony. *Aztec Times*. New York: Simon and Schuster Books for Young Readers, 1997.

McNeese, Tim. *The Great Wall of China*. San Diego: Lucent, 1997.

Millar, Heather. *The Kingdom of Benin in West Africa*. New York: Marshall Cavendish, 1997.

Morley, Jacqueline, and Mark Peppé. *A Renaissance Town*. New York: Peter Bedrick, 1998.

Schomp, Virginia. *Japan in the Days of the Samurai*. New York: Marshall Cavendish, 2001.

Sonneborn, Liz. *The New York Public Library Amazing Native American History*. New York: John Wiley, 1999.

Spence, David. *Michelangelo and the Renaissance*. New York: Barron's, 1997.

Tanaka, Shelley. *Lost Temple of the Aztecs*. New York: Hyperion, 1998.

Wood, Tim. *The Renaissance*. New York: Viking, 1993.

ON-LINE INFORMATION*

http://www.wsu.edu/~dee/REN/
GALLERY.HTM
A list of various artists from the Italian
Renaissance and samples of their work.

http://es.rice.edu/ES/humsoc/Galileo/
People/medici.html
A site with information on the Medici
family and the Italian peninsula during
the fifteenth and sixteenth centuries.

http://www.ibiblio.org/expo/1492.exhibit/
Intro.html
An exhibit sponsored by the Library of
Congress, this site examines the contacts
between American people and Europeans
from 1492 to 1600.

http://www.departments.bucknell.edu/
russian/history.html
Collection of websites about Russian
history.

http://www.discovery.com/stories/history/
greatwall/ming.html
Brief overview of the Ming dynasty.

http://www.wsu.edu:8080/~dee/
OTTOMAN/OTTOMAN1.HTM
Information on the history of the
Ottoman Empire.

http://www.nmafa.si.edu/
Website for the Smithsonian National
Museum of African Art

http://www.indians.org/welker/aztec.htm
Summary of Aztec peoples and culture,
with links to other sites about the Aztec.

http://www.sscf.ucsb.edu/~ogburn/inca/
An introduction to the history of the
Inca empire.

http://jin.jcic.or.jp/museum/menu.html
The Virtual Museum of Traditional
Japanese Art. This site includes information on the crafts, performing arts, and
martial arts of Japan.

*Websites change from time to time. For
additional on-line information, check with
the media specialist at your local library.*

ABOUT THE AUTHOR

Virginia Schomp gradu-
ated from Penn State
University with a degree
in English Literature.
She has written more
than thirty books for
adults and young readers,
on topics including world and U.S. history,
biographies, careers, and dinosaurs.
Ms. Schomp has written two titles in the
Benchmark Books CULTURES OF THE PAST
series: *The Ancient Greeks* and *Japan in
the Days of the Samurai.* She lives in New
York's Catskill Mountain region with her
husband, Richard, and their son, Chip.

INDEX